Project Management

Tips on Rescuing a Project in Trouble

By: Fred Mercado

Table of Contents

Introduction

This book is meant to help any project manager with problems that they may find themselves having when it comes to dealing with the projects that their boss gives them. You may find that time, cost, or scope of the project is keeping you from reaching your full potential for your project. Believe it or not, this isn't just you having these issues. A lot of project managers have this issue.

The goal is to find the proper balance of time and the most effective way to get the project done without costing your company an arm and a leg. We will be discussing how you can properly manage your time, cost, and scope of your project, as well as some of the important principles from PMI.

There are many different things in this book that may cause you to scratch your head because they do not make sense at first. Stop and reread what is written. Sometimes it is easiest if you apply what you are reading to what you already do as a project manager.

By the end of this book, you should be able to find your job is easier and the quality of your work better than before as well as ways that you will be able to save your projects from certain failure should they begin to spiral in that direction.

Chapter 1: How to be a Good Project Manager

A project manager is usually a professional position in which a single person has the responsibility of doing all the planning as well as gathering of tools and even the execution of a project for any domain of engineering or any other field. The person who is in the project manager position tends to be the first point of contact when it comes to any issues that there are on the project. This also includes any discrepancies that the heads of the departments find. The project manager is the person every problem goes through before any issue has to be escalated to someone else.

In order to be a successful project manager, you will be required to balance art and skills. If you are new to being a project manager, the contents of this book will only give you a mere taste of what is going to be coming your way and what is going to be expected of you. However, if you are already a project manager, talk to other project managers so that you can improve your skills. Also, read research and practice.

If you stick with it, you can find the job to be very rewarding. But, first you need to be able to understand some of the more complex issues that you'll face as a project manager. As we've said, this is not an easy job and definitely not for the faint of heart.

If you are not a certified PMP through the Project Management Institute, and it looks like many projects are in your future, I highly suggest that you study the PMBOK guide and attend classes to help you gain this valuable certification. More information on this can be found at www.pmi.org

Things to Keep in Mind to Avoid Project Failure:

- You will become stressed at this job because you are attempting to please everyone, which is normal.

- You need to remember the most important person you want to keep happy is your client.

- You also want to keep your team happy as well because they are the ones doing the work.

Chapter 2: Time Management

Time management can be hard for anyone in everyday life, let alone someone who has deadlines that they have to meet. As a project manager you are doing several different jobs at once and can tend to lose track of the time deadlines. The important thing is to remember is that you need to manage your time in order to make sure that the projects all get done on their own deadline. Following these steps will help you to avoid future failures in your projects.

1. **Create a Plan:** A plan should have milestones in which you are able to reach in specific time periods. Write your plan out so that you can see exactly what it is that you need to do and when you need to have it done by. Seeing your plan written out and being able to cross things off will help to keep you on track.

2. **Remember the 80/20 Rule:** This rule goes by the idea that you should do twenty percent of any work that you can while producing eighty percent of the benefit of the whole job. Essentially you are focusing on twenty perfect of the project activities that matter.

So in the end only twenty percent of the activity you

do is important and therefore will produce eighty percent of your results. Therefore, you need to make sure you focus on the activities that are important to what you are trying to do.

3. **Not just Status Updates:** The best policy is to not hold meetings where you are just telling what updates everyone has. Ultimately these meetings are nothing more than a waste of valuable time that could be spent working on the project. Any meetings that you do have should instead focus on the projects risks, opportunities, and issues.

   Brainstorm as a team rather than as an individual. Make sure your meetings only last around an hour and stick to the agenda. Also, make sure to take any big issues off line so that your meeting does not become over run with the technical issues that may not have anything to do with specific members of the team. Instead, hold focus groups so that you can talk to the members that are affected so that you can find solutions.

4. **Don't Micro-manage:** It is not necessary for the project manager to be involved in things like coding. This is for your team of developers to deal with, not you. If they have any issues, they will come to you. Just let your team do their job because that is why you hired them.

5. **Do not do the Work:** Your job is to manage your teams that are doing the work, not to do the work yourself. If you get involved in doing the work, you may end up creating problems for your team and setting your project back. You'll find that even as the deadlines for your project grow ever closer, you will be more and more tempted to jump in and get the work done so that you reach the deadline successfully. Do not do it!

   This is very important to avoid so that you do not set your project back as stated above. Instead, trust that your team will get the project done on time and turned into you so that you are able to turn it into the appropriate people.

6. **Create a To-do List:** Technology can actually end up distracting you from what you need to get done.

This is why you need to create a to do list so that you can stay focused on what needs to be done. This will also help to make you feel like you have accomplished something for the day that is part of your project rather than sitting around while your team does all the work. Even though your team is doing the work, what you are doing is equally as important as what they are doing.

Chapter 3: Project Costs and Avoiding Failure

The cost of a project can actually set back a project. However, there are ways that you can lower or maintain the cost of your project without sacrificing the quality of your project, making project failures less likely.

It is important to remember every project you do is going to have costs, there is no way that you are going to be able to avoid this. Your computer is a cost, and even the labor of your team is going to end up being a cost for the client. Even if you have gotten halfway through a project and have noticed that it is on a downward spiral, getting on top of these aspects of the project will turn it back around and help you save it.

Ideas for Saving your Project by Managing Project Costs:

- **Take Notes:** It is a good idea to write down all the costs so that you are able to try and find competitive prices for the things that you need, and in doing this, you may even find lower cost of what can be spent in fulfilling the project.

- **Keep the Budget without Sacrificing Quality:** In most cases, a project will have a projected budget that you will be forced to stay within. Finding good, but lowered cost of labor and other equipment that is needed for the job but staying within budget is key.

    You also need to remember that you do not want to lowball yourself and end up with a crappy project all because you were trying to save some money. Good quality is what is going to keep your client coming back for more projects in the future.

- **Be Prepared:** There will always be problems that are going to arise such as with a supplier or even a team member. For these, companies tend to have what is known as a contingency amount that is built into the project budget in order to make sure everything is covered. However, planning for such events is going to help you stay within the budget that you have been given.

Just because you meet the project schedule does not always mean that you have met the project budget, but the chances that you did are exponentially greater. If you find that your budget is blown, you will most likely find that your schedule is blown too and the time for the project to be turned in is either there or has come and gone and your client has left to find someone who could do what they wanted.

Sometimes you may find that your client is going to have you redo the project but without the cost that the originally gave you. This means that you are fixing your mistakes for free. Above all else, make sure you manage your scope. The scope is something we will be discussing in the next chapter.

Chapter 4: The Scope

The word scope holds two different meanings in the field of project management. Let's review the differences between them to give us a clearer picture on saving projects in trouble.

- **Project Scope:** Project Scope is the work that needs to be done in order to deliver a product, service, or result within the specified features and functions that you were given via your client.

  It is important to notice that the project scope is geared more towards the work that you will actually be doing in order to get the project done (the hows);

- **Product Scope:** Product Scope is the features and functions that will characterize a product, service, or even result. Your product scope is more towards how the product will function in the end (the whats).

Either way, the scope is a way of getting the information that is required in order to start a project. This includes the features of the project in order to meet its stakeholder's requirements. Should your requirements not be completely defined by your client, or if there is no effective change control to your project, scope or requirement creep may ensue.

The entire purpose of scope is to define what your project will include as well as the process in which you will carry out the project. There are ultimately three steps that you need to know in order to do scope planning. You can also instate these actions when you notice your project is taking a nosedive, to give it a good chance of picking back up and succeeding.

Collect Requirements: You need to determine the needs as well as the expectations of the key project stakeholders so that you can meet the project objectives properly.

- These requirements will ensure that your project will be a success.

- In order to gather the proper requirements, it is important to have interviews, focus groups, and workshops with your stakeholder as well as your team and even the focused group of people that the project is going to be geared towards.

- If you use these approaches, you will be able to gather the requirements that you need from the different project stakeholders so that you can do your project properly the first time.

Define Scope: Now that you have all the requirements needed, you can then develop the project scope statement.

- This will provide a detailed description of everything that should be included in the project. Some of the critical items that should be addressed are: product scope description, acceptance criteria, exclusions, deliverables, constraints, as well as the assumptions.

- After you have this done, make sure to run it by your client and make sure everything that is included is included so that the team knows the basis for their project.

Create the Work Breakdown Structure: This is the final step in getting your project started.

- You will need to break down the project into more deliverable and more manageable components. For example, say you are responsible for setting up a conference for the newest product that your company has created. You're going to want to handle the venue of where the conference will be held.

- So, in order to break down the venue into more manageable pieces, you're going to want to identify the best possible venue, then book that venue based on the conference dates.

- Next will come the power, sound equipment, chairs and tables, then the catering if you are in need of it.

- Notice that each of these is a smaller piece of a much larger puzzle that you are attempting to solve. It also puts it to where you're not stressing about everything at once.

  <u>Scope Control:</u> This is process in which you will manage the scope of your project so that if anything changes, you will be able to handle it in a controlled way. This would imply that you arc going to need to set up what is known as a change control process.

- Essentially it would be great if you were able to make sure that your scope wouldn't change once it was agreed upon, however, that will never be able to happen.

- Unforeseen events will always arise and force you to change your plan. But, should the changes be taken care of in a controlled manner, it won't be such a bad thing to have to change your scope.

- If the changes are not controlled, that is what is known as a scope creep. Getting a handle on this will turn your failing project back around.

- Controlled changes will come in the form of a formal change request. This request should be analyzed so that the impact to the project can be determined (this includes the impact to the schedule and budget as well as the quality of the project).

- Remember that your client needs to be involved in any changes that are made so that they can then decide if they accept the changes or not. If they do accept, then you will be the one to make sure your team is updated on the changes so that the project is done properly.

Scope Verification: This will be where your client will review the project that is delivered to them in order to make sure that what they have asked for has been delivered based on the requirements that they gave you.

- Your ability to perform the project management scope planning, control, and verification is going to be vitally important to ensure that your project was indeed successful.

- There are many places on the web that you can go in order to research more about the process of project scope management as well as ways you can improve in this area.

Chapter 5: Overall Quality

Quality of the project is obviously going to affect if the client is going to come back to you or not. Of course, you're going to want to do your best and may be asking yourself how are you going to do that if you're constricted by so many things.

First of all, take a deep breath and remember that any one project is not the end of the world. Just because a client complains about a way that you did something does not mean that you will never get another client again, it simply means that you did something they did not approve of.

What to do to Maintain Overall Quality and Avoid or Improve Project Failure:

- **Ask Directly:** If you find this happening to you, ask your client to point out where they feel you failed them on their project.

- **Meet with the Team:** Once they have done this, have a meeting with your team and let them know what has happened and then brainstorm on ways that you could have done it better. Remember that you're only as strong as your weakest link.

- **Find the Specifics of the Issue:** Should you find that one of your team members is the reason that you are constantly getting complaints about the quality of work done by your team, go to that specific team member and try to help them.

  You do not want to receive a bunch of bad reviews on your work because then you may end up not getting as good as clients as you want to get.

- **Remember the Whole:** Work with your team to better as a whole not just as an individual. You didn't do all the work alone so there is no reason that you should be taking all the credit.

  As the project manager, it is your responsibility that you double check your teams work to make sure that the client is actually getting what it is that they want and that your team is delivering the best work that they possibly can.

It is better to do it right the first time than to have to redo it until it is finally done right. If your team has any questions about their quality of work, make sure that you make time to talk to them and walk them through anything that they might not be understanding. If you cannot give them a clear answer, then go to your client and ask your client to explain exactly what it is that they are wanting.

You should always be doing the best work that you possibly can in order to ensure that your client is happy. A happy client is going to keep coming back and even bring you more customers because they are pleased with your work.

One way that you can ensure that your client is happy and to avoid having to waste time fixing mistakes, it is a good practice to give your client updates through the course of the project. This also helps because your client can see your progress as well as tell you what they think of the quality of your work.

As mentioned before, think quality over quantity in most cases. Your client is usually paying big money to be able to have this project completed. Unless specifically stated, always remember your quality.

Chapter 6: Why Projects Fail and How to Avoid it

There are several things that could end up causing your project to fail. Some of these reasons are not going to be your fault, they can end up falling on your client or your upper management. There are reports that say only twenty-six percent of all projects are successful. If we look at that number, then that means, seventy-four percent of all projects actually end up failing. Looking at it, that is a rather alarming number of projects that are failing.

Some companies invest in efforts that are meant to foster communication. Others even invest in newer and better computer systems all in an effort to prevent themselves from failing.

The sad truth is, it really doesn't matter what you do, you will always have projects that are going to fail. The key is to identify where you failed and fix it. Here are some of the top reasons as to why most projects actually fail, and what to do about it.

Senior Management Meddling:

Many project managers actually complain about senior management meddling in their projects. In order to prevent this, a lot of project managers actually go to hiding their information about their projects from their boss.

In doing this, they use summary level reports that they then coordinate major project efforts while senior management is on vacation or otherwise occupied. While creative, this does not actually solve the problem. Some reasons that management tends to meddle is that they are not sure of what else they are supposed to do, they are unsure of how the project is going, or, they have some specific experience in areas of the project and cannot let go.

If you want management to not meddle, ask yourself these two important questions:
1. Why would they be unsure about the project?

2. Have you issued any reports or held any meetings?

If you answered yes to either question, then there could be something missing from this picture that management sees but you don't. Therefore, your best bet is to communicate with management and see if you are missing something.

What to Do to Fix it:

- **Get More Information:** You should ask your management what you need to do in order to make them feel more comfortable about the project. Ask the manager what they would like to see in project progress reports.

- **Keep them Posted:** Tell them about the progress of the project as well as any changes that have come from the client.

- **Enact a Review Schedule:** You can even set up a review schedule before you start your project. This will help you to set up a way for you to work with your management on any issues that shall arise while you work on the project.

- **Involve your Manager:** If you find that your manager actually has some experience in the project, ask yourself if they would be useful in working on it. So, if they end up having more experience than someone on your team, allow the manager to work on the project with you. As a project manager, it is your job to take any and all help that you can find.

Finally, if you believe that your manager is meddling is because they are unsure of what they are supposed to do, ask yourself why. Many people move into a management position because they were good at what they used to do. Therefore, their new promotion can end up calling for a different set of skills that they have yet to master or are attempting to gather.

Relax and work with your manager instead of against them. This could end up helping them in their management role. The success of your project could depend on how well you handle your manager meddling.

Unrealistic Schedules:

It is very often that a client or even manager will give you an end date that may be impossible for you to actually meet. Should or should I say when this occurs, do not argue that "you feel" or "it seems" that it is not enough time for you to complete the project as many project managers do. Instead, use tools that will make it to where you can prove that the date is unrealistic.

Many times these dates are given because of a delay in authorizing the project, the project has problems that are causing it to delay, management believes that the only way to keep the team in line is to give them strict deadlines. There are changes in the competition or the marketplace, or even that the project is at the tail end of a series of projects.

What to Do to Fix it:

- **Avoid Deadlines Until you Plan:** It is suggested that as a project manager ignore the deadline until they actually begin the planning for the project. In order to plan the project, you will be breaking down the project and seeing the ultimate structure and network diagramming. At this point in time you can then determine the critical path or length of time that you need in order to complete the project.

- **Identify Potential Issues:** Once you have completed this, you can then compare the resulting schedule to the actual required completion date. Should there happen to be a difference, prepare the options that you may need to meet in order to meet the date that you are required to meet.

- **If Necessary, Make an Impact Analysis:** This will involve the use of network diagrams in order to crash or even fast track the tasks that need to be done by adding resources, making more tasks occur at the same time, and even deleting the scope work. After doing all this, you can then use the resulting schedule to prove to your management that there is a problem with the schedule that they have set for you.

You will do this by showing them that the scope work required will actually translate to a more realistic completion date that you have already calculated in the work that you did above. Make sure to use a high level work breakdown structure as well as the network diagram so that you can illustrate your point more clearly. Ultimately, the change in due date is going to be up to your management, no matter how good your argument is. Just remember that the best way to prevent project failure is to not allow your management to give require an unrealistic due date out of you.

If you cannot prevent this from happening, then you need to include options that deal with the project plan. A poor project manager will wing their plan and instead of using the entire two months that he had to complete the project, will complete it in the last three weeks before the deadline. The thing you have to think about is, how well will your team respond to this being done to them every time you come across a tight deadline?

Failure to Understand the Impact of Changes:

This becomes a problem when the client or management asks for a "small" change to the scope of the project and does not expect the corresponding change that will happen to the schedule, cost, and several other factors.

The project is carefully balanced based on the time, cost, quality, risk, and performance. If you let this problem happen, then the possibility of you being successful is going to drop dramatically. Therefore, the solution is extremely similar to the solution that you created for the unrealistic time schedule.

There is a lack of knowledge about the triple constraint, the project manager will never communicate that the changes of the scope will indeed affect other areas of the project, also the project manager did not plan their project using the project management tools therefore is unable to provide the proof needed to show management and the client what happens when the scope changes.

What to Do to Fix it:

- **Create an Organized Chart:** By using the tools of work for project managers so that you can have a breakdown structure and network diagram that they need in order to prove what the changes will do to the project.

- **Make the Client Aware:** You can also tell your client how the changes will affect your project and that you are helping to attempt to prevent them, before you even start the project, make sure that your client knows any and all changes will have a major impact on the project, respond to any request that your client has with a detailed impact analysis, and allow your client to have a role in planning the project so that they can see what the changes will do should they happen to want a change later on.

Miscommunication of Scope:

There tends to be a miscommunication when it comes to the scope of work. Which makes it a difference between how management or even your client will perceive the project and what your project team will believe it to be. Some of the biggest reasons that there are miscommunications are because there is poor communication occurring between the parties that are involved in the planning as well as the ones who actually make the decisions, the project charter simply does not exist, the right people are not involved when it comes to scope work, or simply because the scope work was never approved.

What to Do to Fix it:

As a project manager there are things that you can do in order to prevent the miscommunications from happening. But first you need to realize that this isn't just a problem, but a big issue that can cause their project to fail.

- **Keep Everyone in the Know:** One of the most effective ways that has proven to make an impact is to walk through the scope of work line by line with all parties from the very beginning.

  This practice will actually decrease any project changes by sixty percent!

- **Provide Extra Details:** In addition to doing this, you can also attempt to spend a little more time developing a detailed charter. Create a detailed scope description and have it approved by both management and client, make the first phase of your project the requirements validation phase.

- **Step-by-Step:** Walk through the scope with all parties during several parts of the project in order to make sure everything is still on track, explain to your team the importance of not making any changes, ask your client what they expect for when their project is completed, create a scope change process.

- **Make Agreements:** Make sure your team members the duty of informing you of any inadvertent changes made, identify your client's deliverables, require your client and management to sign off on any changes, make sure your client is happy as you present different parts of the projects through the process, and ensure that you are involved in selling the work to your client.

<u>No Risk Management:</u>

Risk management is actually the least understood tool of being a project manager. This is also one area in which many people do not know that they do not understand. The risk management process should involve:

- An in depth analysis as well as a formal analysis for both good and bad things that could end up happening in order for the project to work.

- Detailed plans on how to find a way to prevent the bigger risks. Should you be able to come up with reasons that the project failure occurs, you are learning!

What to Do to Fix it:

Some reasons that there is no risk management is because there is a lack of support for the time that risk management activities would take, lack of knowledge when it comes to risk management, lack of management support for the time needed to plan the project, as well as the belief that risk management needs little to no attention. Since there is such a lack of knowledge when it comes to risk management, the steps needed in order to handle the risks comes at last minute.

- **Prioritize Training:** Essentially it is up to you as the project manager to get the proper training and then to help train the management of risk management. Sadly, there is very little access to risk management training and currently there are no books that are useful.

- **Get Educated on the Subject:** If you are looking for material to read on risk management, your best bet is going to be "A Guide to the Project Management Body of Knowledge" as well as the articles that are published monthly and quarterly.

- **Identify and Communicate Dangers:** Other than that, you can inform everyone of past impacts of not analyzing the potential problems and ways to avoid them, add risk management to project management procedures (even if you are unsure of what risk management is, look at the good and bad that can happen to the project).

You can also make a list of all problems that your team has had on past projects, involve any experts you may know of to your team, and obtain any and all training you can on risk management.

No Historical Data:

Historical data is used in order to identify any risks you may run into, improve your estimating, identify your tasks that need to be done, and create a work breakdown structure. But, the biggest thing you will find is that no one uses the historical data even if it is available.

Any historical data that you have from past projects can be used to make a list of any risks you may run into, work breakdowns and structures, sample project plans, management plans, and even communication plans, tasks and their estimated time and cost, and any lessons that were learned from the project such as where it was successful and where it failed.

What to Do to Fix it:

Historical data should be kept companywide so that you have a rather large pool of information that you can pull from on your projects. however, the biggest reason that the data is not kept is because no one knows how to store it or manage it.

- **Do your Own Research:** Instead of waiting for management to find and give you the data that you need, go find it on your own. Use your team to help you get this data so that you have a wider range of data that you can pull from.

- **Create a Database:** If it has not already been done, create a historical database in which the information will be stored so that it can be used later on. Some other options that you might have are to ask any other project managers about their data (you can even go outside your company).

- **Salvage by Starting Anew:** Start a new project with data accumulation effort and make sure you involve your client and your team, read the project management articles and any other publications that you can get your hands on.

- **Stay Curious:** Ask your management to make a special effort to talk to other managers and see if you can obtain their data, explain that having the data will take less effort on each project, and finally should you find some valuable information, point out the benefit of having the historical database. You will not only be helping yourself bit those around you.

Like with anything you are going to learn from the past better than anything. In order to know where you are going, you must first know where you've been.

To Avoid Failure, be Aware of the Following:

- Overselling.

- A lack of project management training.

- Projects that are planned without the project manager.

- Inexperience.

- No change control system.

- Turnover rates.

- Not following the schedule and budget that was created during the planning process.

- Inappropriate contract types being used.

- Project teams not being involved in the planning.

- A lack of effective communication.

- No system made for controlling the project.

- A focus on Gantt or bar charts being used as the only project control tool.

Ultimately, there are many factors that are going to wreak havoc on your project and possibly make it fail. The only thing you can do is to make sure you are prepared for the risks and know ways to be able to work around them. There really is no formal training when it comes to the risks that you're going to run into.

Take each project as a new challenge. But, don't forgot about problems you have run into in the past. You may find yourself running into them again and if that is the case, you need to know how to fix the problem quickly and efficiently so you can move on to completing the project in a timely manner.

Chapter 7: Signs a Project is in Trouble and What to Do

As any project manager knows, projects can take unexpected turns when you least expect it. Sometimes this can be avoided, but simply isn't because your job is stressful and you may just blow it off thinking that your project is going to be perfectly fine and that it's just a bump in the road.

However, if you begin to see certain signs within your team or project, you need to pay attention to them or else your project is going to end up failing in the long run and you may end up not being able to solve it. Later on in the book we will give you a few ways that you can revive a project as well how to get it back on track. But for now, let's look at signs that your project may be heading towards failure.

"What problem are we trying to solve?"

At the point in time that you hear your team asking this question, it should make you realize that there has either been a lack of communication or there are questions that need to be asked and answered but have not been. But, if you hear your client ask this question, you now have proof that your project is on shaky ground because your client obviously is not getting the results that they were hoping for.

If your team does not know what the projects agenda is or they have lost sight of what your client wants, you're going to find it harder to inspire your team to work harder on the project or to even be able to brainstorm new ideas for it.

What to Do to Fix it:

- **Don't Make Assumptions:** Don't just assume that the projects purpose is obvious, it may be obvious to you, but not to your team.

- **Ask Questions to Stay on the Same Page:** Make sure your team knows what the purpose of the project is and make sure you communicate clearly with everyone on your team to ensure everyone is on the same page.

- **Over-communicate:** Too much is never enough. Remember, your project is not going to fail just because you over-communicate. Your project is going to fail due to lack of communication.

Avoid the Idea that Failure is not an Option:

Do not instill this way of thinking into your team members. This kind of attitude is what is going to keep your team from hearing all the information that they need to hear as well as make them believe that they cannot come to you with questions about things that could possibly go wrong.

If you cut off the line of communication, then your team is not going to have clear communication with you and could lose sight of the purpose of the project. In fact, having this kind of environment is going to increase the chances of your team failing despite the fact that they do not want to.

Management changes

In the shuffle of people leaving and entering the company during projects may make it slightly harder for your team to be able to accomplish what they need to accomplish. It is possible that new upper management may not adopt all the previous manager's priorities. When the internal dynamic changes, it there is a temporary lack of communication between everyone in the company.

Ultimately, the change in management or management being inconsistent is what is going to confuse people and lead a project to fail.

What to Do to Fix it:

- **Communicate Effectively:** If you find that your company is going through a management change, keep your team updated but also let them know that you are still there to answer any questions that they have in order to make sure that the project succeeds.

- **Solve Problems Early on:** Any problems with management that you end up having can be solved as they arise.

Office politics:

This is something that is hard to avoid no matter where you work. However, the biggest red flag that you need to keep your eye out for is when your corporate politics and project goals begin to conflict. These politics don't necessarily have to come from your company either, but they can come from your client. While it is impossible to keep politics out of the office or out of your client's office, you can keep them out of your project.

What to Do to Fix it:

- **Keep the Team Involved:** Make sure to keep your team focused but in the loop as to what is going on. Do not let them lose focus on what they are trying to accomplish.

- **Re-focus the Team if Necessary:** Do not let the happenings around the office fracture your team with the "he said, she said" that will no doubt happen.

- **Know what you're Dealing with Ahead of Time:** Make sure your team is strong and able to withstand anything that may be thrown their way. Your project is the most important thing that you need to keep your focus on.

Over-budget with Overtime

It is very easy to wear your team out with working overtime as they attempt to get a project done on time. This can especially be tiresome when the plan for the project is flawed and no one has bothered to try and fix it. Also, as your team tries to work through a project, no one is necessarily paying attention to the budget and then before you know it, you're over budget. Once this happens, the project ending well is not necessarily going to happen.

If your team is constantly working overtime, that is your biggest sign that you have taken on more than your team can actually accomplish. Everyone wants to believe that their team is the best, but just to prove it does not mean that you have to take on huge projects that your team is not equipped to handle. The biggest failure for this is going to come when your resources are now being spread too thin or not getting used at all because you have hit your budget cap and are not allotted any more money.

What to Do to Fix it:

- **Focus on Quality Before Beginning:** If you keep putting the quality of your work off, then what is going to happen when you forget about the quality of your project and then end up turning it over to the client without adding in that quality?

- **Always Keep Quality in Mind:** Focus on your quality as you work on the project. The less you have to rush at the end means the more time that you end up having to fix any mistakes and possibly add in anything that you may have not thought of before.

Quality is a big thing that is going to determine whether or not your client is happy with the project or not. If it is poor quality, then the chances of you getting that client to do return work with you is very slim.

Procrastination:

Someone on the team will always end up suffering from lack of interest or commitment to the project and this will end up bringing the team down because that particular team member is not pulling their weight to make sure that the project is getting done.

If your client is the one that ends being the one that holds a lack of interest in the project, then you'll be finding yourself needing to readjust it to where the client is interested in their own order once more. When someone is not showing an interest they will begin to not show up for the project meetings or they will be passive aggressive when it comes to anything that they actually participate in.

What to Do to Fix it:

- **Keep the Team Interested:** Talk to your team member or client and find ways to get them interested again so that you are not forcing your team members to pick up where they are slacking.

- **Set and Adhere to a Strict Schedule:** Making a strict schedule from the start is crucial, but if your project starts failing, it's never too late to start. Procrastination is only going to end up putting your team behind schedule and you may not make your deadline. Not only that, but you could end up going over the deadline or worse, turning in a half completed project.

Chapter 8: How to Save a Failing Project

As we stated in the previous chapter, there are many reasons as to why a project is going to fail. Sometimes the reason a project fails can be fixed rather quickly by simply talking to your manager. Other times it takes you doing research and placing the proof in front of your manager and client so that they can make the proper decision that will not harm the project. However, there are other ways that you can save a failing project that may not be that simple to save.

To quote Ralph Young, Steven Brady, and Dennis Nagle the authors of *How to Save a Failing Project: Chaos to Control*. "Poor project results are all too common. We often hear about projects that are canceled, go over budget, are completed late, or deliver less functionality than promised. Customers are dissatisfied, users are disappointed, and project staff are frustrated and overworked. Program and project managers may even lose their jobs."

The above quote essentially means that no matter what, you're going to run into problems that will set your project back or cause it to begin failing. The results can change based on how you react to the downward spiral that your project will begin to take as it begins to fail so that you can turn a failure, into a success.

- **Take Responsibility:** First you need to stop playing the blame game: It is very easy to get caught up in pointing fingers at who caused what portion of the project to fail. However, if you want to know the honest truth, blame ultimately begins at the top of the food chain.

  Instead of pointing fingers and placing blame on everyone, try and help be part of the solution. Step up and come up with solutions that are going to help the project instead of hinder it.

- **Focus on the Facts:** Your best friend while a project begins to fail should be the real data that is collected as you move through working on the project. You need to get into the details of exactly what has gone wrong and at what stage this happened. Ultimately, once you have that information, you can be able to answer why that happened.

- **Find the "Why" Behind the Failure:** Getting to the bottom of the problems with a project is much like when you peel an onion. You're peeling apart the layers of the problem and trying to get down to the bottom of *why* something happened.

At the point in time you have figured out why the problem occurred, you are now at a point in time that you can figure out how to solve the problem as well as ways you can use to prevent the same problem from happening in the future.

- **Avoid Making Assumptions:** If you are unable to verify an opinion or assumption as to how the problem occurred, then it is best to let that one go because you need to focus on the facts that you can physically see and prove. If you let yourself get caught up in all the assumptions that can go on, then you're never going to truly find out the solution.

  As humans it is truly easy for you to jump to the fastest conclusion that makes sense to you, and that will end up causing more problems to arise other than what you are already trying to solve.

- **Use the Same Team:** The only time that you should really change someone on the team is if your project begins to take a new course and you need someone who has the specific set of skills that you are looking for. However, if your goal is the same as before, there is no sense in firing anyone from the team.

- **Keep an Eye on the Team:** Even if your management is not seeing the results that they want as you use the same people that you began to project with, you do not need to get rid of anyone. Often times it is not the team that is the problem, but what the team is doing.

There are often times that projects will fail because they are understaffed in areas that are ultimately important to the project. It can even fail because the project manager did not think through the plan properly and break up the project as they should have into more manageable pieces for their team to deal with.

Make sure that the scope of your project is defined and that your team understands what is going to happen in the end. Set goals for your team to reach rather than attempting to get the project done all at once and overwhelming your team with a huge project that has to be done. Also, don't micromanage. Micromanaging will only slow your team down in the long run.

- **Remember to Over-communicate:**
  Communication is key: it is important that your team fully understand what your project is going to be in the end as well as why they are working on the project. Keeping everyone on the same page is key and the only way that is going to happen is if you communicate everything with them.

  One of the biggest reasons any project will fail is because of the lack of communication. Now, this is not necessarily your fault as a project manager, sometimes it happens because members of your team get so caught up in their work that they tend to forget to check in on what the rest of the team is doing and if everything is going to work together properly.

One very important thing that you need to keep in mind is that you need to look at your resources and decide if it is ultimately helping to serve the goals of getting the project done properly. In order for your strategy to work, you need to make sure that your people and technology are the best for the job.

Chapter 9: How to Get a Project Back on Track

You're trying to save your project or have saved it and found that it has managed to get off track. This is a common occurrence after a project has begun to show signs of failing. As a project manager, it is your job to keep the project on track and keep it going in the direction that you need it to go in so that it gets done on time and properly.

As we've stated before, we don't want to micromanage your team because then they will feel as if they are under a microscope constantly and may not produce the best results. If your team is not giving you the best results that they absolutely can, then your project is not going to meet your client's expectations.

So in order to get your project back on track, follow some of these simple steps:

1. **Assess the situation:** Gather all the data that you possibly can from your project in order to make the proper decision without harming the project in the long run. During this part of the process you will find that you are going to have more questions than answers, and that is okay because you're trying to find

out how to get the project back on track.

It is vitally important that you make sure that you are asking the proper questions in order to make that happen. You need to get the most accurate picture of what has happened to the project that you can.

2. **Be Honest about Where you Are:** No positive changes can be made if you cannot be honest about where your project is. Realistically assess the information and figure out what needs to be done, including all of the hard work and details.

3. **Start Over:** Being a good project manager often means knowing when it's time to start a project over. There is no shame in abandoning a method that isn't working and developing something new.

Some key questions that you may want to ask are:

- How willing is your client or manager going to be if you propose a change in the budget, the scope, or even the due dates?

- Is the functionality of the product going to be where it needs to be by the time that the due date comes around?

- What is the progress of the project?

- What still needs to be completed?

- And, how critical is it that you have the entire project due by the delivery date?

One of the problems that you may find you have an issue with getting answers to is how willing your client or manager would be to changes. This is because there are going to be people and possibly even politics that are involved in the project that you are working with. You may even run into the ideology that your client isn't going to want to change anything unless it will directly benefit them and they would rather the project fail than to change something that will not help them. But, in order to help save the project, there may be things that *have* to be changed despite how adamant the client is about not changing them.

Just like stated in the previous chapter, you're going to want to figure out where the project began to turn towards failure. Not only do you need to get the data but also try and get some opinions from your team and see if what they think happened matches up with the data. Remember that you want solid proof of everything rather than assumptions.

Prepare your team for recovery:

When you're preparing for the recovery of your project you need to make sure everyone is on the same page, from the client, to your boss, to your team. The fact that there is something that needs to be fixed needs to be accepted by all involved so that the problem can indeed be fixed in the best way possible. If someone is not on the same page, then there will be resistance against those on the team who are not against the changes that need to come in order to fix what has happened.

- **Define your Expectations:** At the point in time that you have gotten everyone on board with the change, you'll need to be able to define realistic expectations for what can be delivered based on the time line that you have as well as the current state of the project.

- **Measure your Recovery:** Make sure that you have a way to measure the recover as well as how successful it is. If the metrics that you have currently for the project as it is, you may want to set new metrics for the "new" project. Once these are defined, hold not only your team but yourself accountable to them.

- **Improve the Work Environment:** Alongside with your manager, you need to be able to develop an environment in which your team members feel supported. This can be accomplished by making sure that your team members have realistic goals to reach as well as providing them with the space, equipment, and training that they need in order to push the project towards success.

- **Pay Attention to Success Momentum:** It is also vitally important that you take advantage of any momentum that leans towards success. Make sure you keep all parties involved in the project motivated and engaged in the recovery of the project so that you can ultimately come up with the product that your client wanted in the first place.

Develop a game plan:

A good plan is to look at the recovery of your project as a new project rather than the same project that had spiraled down towards failure.

- **Sit Down with the Team:** In order to do this, it is best that you once again sit down with the client as well as your manager and write out a new scope as well as the new expectations that everyone expects to be delivered.

- **Clarify all Details:** Everything for the "new" project needs to be crystal clear so that you can properly relay the information to your team and avoid failure yet again.

With a new scope, there may be new technologies or other resources that you need in order to make sure the project goes off without a hitch. You may even end up finding out that you'll need to re-staff the project with people who have the proper skills needed to make sure the project is a success.

Maintain Focus:

The biggest goal of having a new scope and a new plan is to make sure that the project **does not** fail again. The fact that it has already failed once will put your team under the microscope a bit when it comes to management. Don't freak out over this because it just means that your team needs to be careful and follow the plan that has been set out.

- **Set New Milestones:** In order to help your team, succeed the second time around, set your milestones at shorter durations so that you can prove that your team is succeeding and it will give you more time that you may need to fix any mistakes that happen to pop up this time around.

You won't feel as rushed as you were before because your team now has the time to correct the mistakes because of the shorter duration they have to reach their milestones.

- **Keep the Team's Needs in Mind:** Although, you may find some team members do not do well under the pressure and you will need to either replace them or help them meet their deadlines. An added bonus is that with the shorter milestones, you will be able to provide your client and management with data points that will help to track the health of the project from the "beginning."

Execute the game plan:

Now you have the plan that you need in order to make the project successful, now it is time to put that plan into action and get the project done. At this point in time, you aren't the only one who is on the hook, neither is your team, but your manager is as well. Everything needs to be in sync the second time around to ensure the success of your project.

- **Leave no Questions Unanswered:** Make sure the new plan has been clearly communicated to your team and that they have no questions. Not only that, but make sure that any questions they do end up coming up against are instantly brought to your attention. If the project begins to spiral like it did the last time, make sure you have a plan for that as well.

- **Hold Team Members Accountable:** Make sure that everyone keeps their own personal agenda out of the project or anything else personal that could end up causing the project to fail yet again.

- **Stay Realistic:** Remember that you're going to have to put forth a lot of effort, commitment, objectivity, as well as focus in order to keep the project on its new track.

Also, don't lose sight over the pressure that everyone is now under. If you thought it was bad before, it is going to be worse now because they are now under the pressure that they have failed once and they could end up failing again. Give your team positive feedback and try and maintain a positive environment. You're going to also need to be able to help your team bond as well as have a way to release any steam that they may have pent up so that they can keep their focus on the project.

At the point in time that your project has been delivered to the client, make sure that you have recognized the effort that each and every one of your team members put in to making the project a success.

Take what you have learned from having to put your project back on track and take it with you to the next project. This will help you to stop other projects from failing. If you notice the warning signs that your project is beginning to fail, you can quickly place these steps into play and recover it before it gets too far out of hand.

Remember, you may not be able to recover every project. Some projects are just going to fail. Don't let these failures take you too far or else you'll begin to see all your projects failing.

Chapter 10: Meetings for Saving a Project

We've talked about ways that a project can fail, signs that a project is failing, and even ways to fix the failure or to get your project back on track. One thing that you may have noticed is the common theme is the theme of communication!

Communication is key when it comes to a team and any project that they are doing. Communication is how they are going to get the project details, find answers to questions to avoid failure, and so on and so forth.

So, what is the biggest way that you as the project manager can keep the lines of communication open in order to avoid failure? The most obvious answer of course is going to be to hold a meeting. A meeting is going to get your entire team together with your manger and the client and be able to keep everyone on the same page.

But, is your meeting actually beneficial to your project? Let's take a look at a few things that you can do in order to help make sure your meetings that you do hold are effective and beneficial to your project.

How to Make Sure your Meetings will Work for Saving a Project:

- **Is your Meeting really Needed?** This should be the first question you as yourself before you even begin to set up any sort of meeting with your team, manager, or client. How much time are you going to be taking from the project in order to talk to everyone that is involved and can that time be made up in work?

  Use your best judgement on if a meeting should be held. Remember that holding a five minute meeting really isn't worth all the time and effort you're going to have to go through in order to make sure everyone can attend.

- **Plan and Structure your Meeting:** This seems like a no brainer, but it's important to remember. Your meeting needs to have structure in order to make sure that it stays on track.

  The best way to do this is to come up with an objective as to why you are holding the meeting. Make sure your team and anyone else who is attending the meeting knows exactly what the agenda is so that they are not surprised by anything that may come up.

- **Keep it Short and to the Point:** Try and keep your meeting as short as possible but not so short that it is a waste of time as we've mentioned before. Try and avoid any meetings that may be contiguous (meetings that are in a row) as those that you want at your meeting will lose anything that they need to know from the first meeting(s) that they attended.

- **Set a Time Limit for the Meeting:** Try and keep your meeting to around thirty minutes. Between thirty minutes to an hour is an idea meeting so that people are able to take what you said and go back to work and apply it. This will also not cut out too much of their work time that is needed in order to make sure that the client's project gets done on time.

- **Choose your Audience Wisely:** do you honestly need your entire team at the meeting? If you only need a specific set of people who are dealing with, say the coding of the program, then only pull them into a meeting rather than your entire team. This will help to avoid putting the project behind schedule.

- **Stay Honest with the Audience:** There's no point in sugar coating facts at the meeting to save a project. The team members are just as much a part of the project as you are and they deserve honesty. This will make saving the project run more smoothly.

- **Stay Appropriate and on Task:** If you need your manager or even the client there, make sure that they are at the meeting to keep things on task.

- **Get Approval:** Any meeting that has to do with a problem that your team has run into or any changes that may need to be made, make sure they are there. You do not need to be changing things without approval from the client or your manager.

- **Organize the Information:** Print out or email out everything that you're going to be going over in the meeting so that your team can be prepared and possibly bring up any information that you may need to know.

- **Start on Time:** As has been mentioned before, you're losing valuable work time when you pull people away for meetings. So, in order to not waste even more time, you need to make sure that your meeting starts when you say it will start. If something happens that holds the meeting up from starting or ending when it should, that is a different story.

But, make sure you do everything within your power to keep the meeting on schedule so everyone can go back to work and get the project done.

- **Keep it Interesting but on Topic:** Have an engaging meeting: make sure that everyone gets something valuable from the meeting. Once again, if they do not take something away from the meeting that will help them in their work, then the meeting was more than likely a waste of their time.

- **Get Everyone to Speak Up:** Encourage your team members to share their opinions and ideas on the project. Brainstorm as a team rather than as an individual so that your team can stay on the same page.

It is important to remember that not everyone is going to want to share their opinion so try and keep the discussion to the room rather than picking on individuals who aren't saying anything. Chances are that they will come to you later so that they can talk to you instead of having to feel as if they are being singled out in a room full of people.

- **Check with the Team:** At the end of the meeting it is important to make sure everyone is still on the same page and that everyone agrees on any new deadlines or ideas that you came up with in order to reach your goal.

- **Keep the Meeting on Track**: Don't lose sight of what the meeting was originally set up to discuss. People are going to try and pull the meeting off track by telling you stories about things that have happened on past projects or whatever else comes to their mind.

  Don't let that happen. It is okay if people voice their opinions but you have an agenda and you need to stick to it as much as you possibly can. Any long winded explanations that you can avoid are better because you'll end up finding that half of your room will mentally drift away from the meeting and yet again you are doing nothing but wasting time.

- **Stay Positive**: Try and focus on the good things that the team has done as well as discussing any issues that have arisen or risks that they see will come from the project. It is important that you know what is going on with the project and that you make your team feel appreciated for the work that they are doing.

- **Keep it about Business:** it is great if you are friends with your team members. But business meetings are not meant for catching up and telling stories of Sally's great aunt whose dog just had puppies.

- **Keep Conflicts Out of it:** At the same time, it is not a time that you need to ambush any individuals for something that they may have (or not have) done. This is also not a time for you to try and resolve any conflicts.

  Problems such as this are meant to be solved outside of the meeting room and more on a one on one basis. The only time any issues should be resolved in a meeting is if there is an issue with the project or if there is an issue with the team as a whole in order to make sure that you are not compromising the projects integrity.

- **Sum up the Information:** When you're closing your meeting, make sure that you reiterated what you originally started the meeting out for. Make sure that your team is on the same page! It is vitally important that everyone has agreed on anything that has been changed. Also, if at all possible, try and end your meeting on a good note (especially if the meeting was not a meeting that was the most positive).

You want your team members to go back to work engaged, enthused, and ready to tackle whatever is next on their list of things to do. This way you're sure you're getting the best quality of work from them rather than them wishing that it was already quitting time.

- **Finish on Time:** Just as you had to start on time, finish on time. Try not to run your meeting over unless you absolutely have to.

If your meeting didn't reach the goals that you wanted, you may need to schedule another meeting or you may need to schedule one on ones with the people that you need to in order to make sure everything is ironed out.

Also, make sure you don't rush the meeting and end up coming up with some conclusion to any issue that has been brought to your attention as then you will be compromising your project and getting your meeting off track; therefore, making your team forget what the meeting was about in the first place.

Chapter 11: Five Principles of a Successful Project Manager

One of the greatest ways to handle a failed project is to use it to become better. If you don't follow this idea, the failure was in vain. Everyone wants to be successful, but there are always going to be steps that you need to take in order to be successful. Success will not just come overnight for anyone no matter who you are. You will have to work at becoming a success, and as always, there are different ways that you can do this. These are just a few principles that others have turned to and found to help them be successful.

- "The Initiating Process Group Consist of those processes performed to define a new project or a phase of an existing project by obtaining authorization to start the project or phase" -A Guide to the Project Management Body of Knowledge Fourth Edition.

Ultimately in order to initiation or begin work on any project you may have, you need to first have a plan and have that plan authorized by the client before you begin to work. In many cases you will find that you have already gone through this process.

However, you may find that it is easier on everyone for you to make sure that every meeting you have is in a centralized location that is easy to get to by all parties involved. You're going to want to keep your meeting business-like, but also fun so that you can keep everyone who is involved interested in the project. In many cases, it is during meetings like this that the best ideas come out and make your project better than it would have been before.

- "The Planning Process Group consists of those processes required to establish the scope of the project, refine the objectives, and define the course of action required to attain the objectives that the project will undertake to achieve." - PMBOK Guide

Planning is something that you're going to be doing throughout your project no matter what stage it is in. Just as we stated before, unforeseen changes will always arise, forcing you to change how you are doing things.

Ultimately during this process, you are going to go over every aspect of the project in order to ensure everyone is on the same page. Not only that, but you are going to want to make sure that you find ways to keep your client happy while you attempt to stay on track and on budget.

The best way to keep your client happy is to do what they ask of you the first time. With some clients this may seem impossible, but if you do it rather than worry about everything else, your client will be pleased that you put their project and needs before anything that could have or did happen.

- "The Executing Process Group consist of those processes performed to complete the work defined in the project management plan to satisfy the project specifications." -PMBOK Guide

Make sure that your team is all on the same page in order to pull the project off successfully. Everyone should know exactly what is needed of them in order for it to all go off without a hitch. Even if one person is not on the same page, you could end up experiencing setbacks as well as multiple other problems that will lead to your project not being as successful as you would like it to be.

It is not necessarily a bad thing if everyone on your team as a check list of things that they are supposed to accomplish in order to help with what they need to do for the project. Your job as the project manager is to make sure that your team knows what it is that they are doing and that they are not left floundering in the dark.

- ""The Monitoring and Controlling Process Group. Those processes required to track, review, and regulate the progress and performance of the project; identify any areas in which change to the plan are required; and initiate the corresponding changes." - PMBOK Guide.

As mentioned above, as the project manager it is your job to monitor the progress and any changes that are going on through your project. You are the one who is monitoring and controlling any processes that are needed in order to ensure that your client gets exactly what it is that they want.

If you are finding that a team member is struggling and unable to keep up with the workload, assign someone else to help them keep up with their work so that it gets done in time. Remember that we said earlier that you do not want to get involved in doing the work yourself because then you are not doing your job and monitoring the progress of the project.

- "The Closing Process Group consists of those processes performed to finalize all activities across all the Process Groups to formally close the project or phase." PMBOK Guide.

So, the project has finally reached its end and you are going over everything to make sure that it all go done the way that the client wanted in order to turn it over to them. As the project manager, you should have been monitoring all the processes throughout the entire project so nothing should come as a surprise to you when you go over the finalized project.

When you do turn over the project to your client, let your team know what the client said. Make sure that you praised them through the entire process so that they feel like all the work that they did is appreciated and that they are valued members of your team.

No matter what you do, you're going to receive feedback on your work. It is up to you that depends on what you do with the negative feedback. You can take it and grow with it or you can let it set you back. My opinion is that your user it to grow and do better the next time around.

Chapter 12: Getting Rid of Distractions

One thing that you may see adds to any failure that your project may have is distractions. Not only can you end up getting distracted but your team can end up getting distracted.

Distractions are going to lead to your project not being done on time or even poor quality of your project. The only way that you can ensure that your team does not get distracted is to try and aid in not being part of those distractions.

The number one distraction for anyone now days is technology. We have our entire world at the tip of our fingers. But, while you're working on a project, the most common technology problems that may arise are going to be emails and new project requests.

No Checking your Email During Work:

If emails are the problem, then close your email down to where you cannot see it while you work. If you need to open your email, that should be the time that you lower your project and check everything at once before getting back to work.

Try and keep any emails to your team to a minimum so that you are not causing them to be distracted by a million different emails from you. Sometimes it is unavoidable to sending an email out, but the one thing you can do is try and keep it to one or two emails while they are working.

Realistically Assess How Much Work you can Handle:

Another distraction can be the project requests that you're bound to get. Make sure that you do not say yes to these requests too quickly or else you're going to end up overwhelming yourself with projects that have to be done. Think if it is realistic for your team to get the project done on time or if it is going to overwhelm them. It is best that you use some sort of system that shows all your projects and the due dates for them.

Plan Ahead to Avoid Distractions:

At the same time, make sure that you plan ahead. You don't want your team having massive amounts of down time so that they are growing bored and not having anything to do. This will cause the productivity of another project to decrease when they do get assigned another project. This can be a distraction for your team because they are looking at all the projects that are there and everything that has to be done and they will lose sight of what they currently need to be doing.

Always Keep the Program in Mind:

Once again, make sure you have some sort of program that shows every project that you have and anything that has to be done on it. Make it accessible to your team so that they can see what is going on and allows them to stay on the same page as you.

And yet again, make sure that your team has a clear view of the details of the project and what needs to be done. Everyone knows that it is hard to shift priorities and if the energy of the work place is scattered, your team productivity will decrease. This is a major distraction because they will end up trying to figure out what the project is truly about.

The Simpler, the Better:

Try and keep everything as simple as possible. The simpler the better therefore the less distractions that you'll have.

Don't tell your team that they can't look at their emails or anything else because then you'll find that they won't be able to communicate with you and having to hold back issues that they find is a distraction in and of itself. Just try and limit the distractions that you cause for your team as well as distractions that you cause for yourself.

Conclusion

Thank you for downloading this book! If you enjoyed this book, please take a few moments to give me a *Book Review on Amazon.* I would greatly appreciate it!

My hope is that this book was able to help you find something new in order to incorporate into your project management. The many different resources that you can use in order to help further your career as a project manager. Some have been listed in this book while there are many others out there that you can use.

If you were able to find one thing in this book that you did not know before, then this book was a success and I hope that what you learned is something that will make you more successful as a project manager.

Being a project manager is not for everyone and can be a stressful job. It is important that if you find yourself slacking in your duties, you hand the reigns over to someone else so that you can refocus and come back to your team with fresh ideas and ways to keep them engaged in their jobs on their projects.

In doing your research you will find that there are many different tools and techniques that you can use. It is your decision on what you use because you're going to have to find what works best for you. However, you're going to have to test which technique you like on different projects. Just remember that you may have a project or several projects that are going to fail. Do not let that failure stop you from what you are trying to do. Keep pushing through and celebrate in the projects that are successful.

You will see that several things were mentioned several times such as the fact that you need to manage any changes that are made to the scope as well as that you do not need to micromanage. On top of all of that, you are now well versed in how to turn a project around once it beings to show signs of failure.

A lot of what you read is common sense to all of us, however it is different when you are in a project manager role. While a lot of this stuff can be applied to the outside world, you need to see the difference in the role at work. Once again, thank you for downloading this book and please leave your review on the major retailer's website in which you bought it.
Good luck!

About the Author

Fred Mercado PMP, is the president of Mercado Consulting; A Consulting company with a focus in the Enterprise and Wireless industry in North America and the Caribbean and Latin America - CALA. He holds an AS Degree in Avionics from Embry-Riddle Aeronautical University, a Bachelor of Science Degree in Business from Excelsior College of New York, and MBA in International Business from American Intercontinental University of Chicago.

Fred is an experienced business executive with over 30 years of professionalism in the business and telecommunication industry. He is a well-known leader and achiever as his expertise expands through domestic and international markets. He has worked in various executive level positions with several well established organizations including his time with Wireless Facilities Inc., Crown-Castle International, MetroPCS, and at McCaw Cellular Communications/AT&T Wireless. Fred also serves as a Board Advisor and technical & business consultant to several companies in the telecommunications industry.

Fred also has several internationally recognized certificates including Project Management Professional (PMP), Corporate Governance (Sarbanes Oxley - SOX) from Tulane University, Negotiations, and Organisational Behaviour, from Heriot-Watt University in the UK and is a certified

Total Quality Management (TQM) Instructor. He has written several industrial papers that gained the attention of many and as an author writing a series of books to share his experience, knowledge and expertise in a bid to further educate, assist and build new leaders. His series covers every aspect in establishing knowledge and expertise in the field of Business, Project Management, and overall Leadership.

You can learn more about Fred by visiting:

www.mercadoconsulting.com

www.fredmercado.com

https://www.linkedin.com/in/fredmercado

Also visit my website at www.thenewleaders.com to join the team of leaders making a difference in today's society.

Bonus:

Subscribe to The New Leaders and receive a free eBook on Leadership.

Visit my site at http://www.thenewleaders.com and join my email list. When you sign up I will send you updates on advancements, news, educational information, and opportunities to help advance your leadership ambitions and skills.

I also have a Free eBook that I will send you upon joining the list. The ebook is full of relevant and extremely useful information on becoming a great leader, and a great source of information to home the leadership skills you already have.

It is free with no strings attached, just my way of thanking you for purchasing my book and joining the league of today influential leaders.

Disclaimer:

The author of this book did all the research that was necessary in order to bring you the most up to date information that will help you. Some of the examples and things that have been stated also come from other project managers that the author personally knows and has gotten to sit in and watch how they do their job.

As mentioned above, being a project manager can be stressful at times. Especially when the job requires you to oversee multiple projects at a time. Do not let the stress affect how you do your job. Take time for yourself so that you do not get your projects confused and end up giving your client the wrong project.

The number one thing that you need to remember is that you need to keep your team and your client happy. If both are not happy, then something is not going right and you need to take a step back and find a new tactic. A team that is not developing the proper quality of product is going to end up losing you clients in the long run and therefore you will end up feeling like you are unable achieve anything.

Listen to your team, listen to your client, and keep your head above the water. That is the most important thing to remember. You are the one who is in charge of the project and the finalization of it. Remember what you have been taught and you should do just fine.

You are going to run into problems no matter how long you end up doing the job, it is important that you do not let these set you back. If you let every small problem set, you back then you will never end up succeeding. It is important that you take your failures and learn from them.

www.ingramcontent.com/pod-product-compliance
Lightning Source LLC
Chambersburg PA
CBHW060408190526
45169CB00002B/809